BOA
EDITIONS LTD

TWO BROWN DOTS

Winner, A. Poulin, Jr. Poetry Prize
Selected by Aimee Nezhukumatathil

TWO BROWN DOTS

POEMS BY

DANNI QUINTOS

FOREWORD BY AIMEE NEZHUKUMATATHIL

A. POULIN, JR. NEW POETS OF AMERICA SERIES, NO. 46

BOA EDITIONS, LTD. ❖ ROCHESTER, NY ❖ 2022

First Edition
22 23 24 25   7 6 5 4 3 2 1

For information about permission to reuse any material from this book, please contact The Permissions Company at www.permissionscompany.com or e-mail permdude@gmail.com.

Publications by BOA Editions, Ltd.—a not-for-profit corporation under section 501 (c) (3) of the United States Internal Revenue Code—are made possible with funds from a variety of sources, including public funds from the Literature Program of the National Endowment for the Arts; the New York State Council on the Arts, a state agency; and the County of Monroe, NY. Private funding sources include the Max and Marian Farash Charitable Foundation; the Mary S. Mulligan Charitable Trust; the Rochester Area Community Foundation; the Ames-Amzalak Memorial Trust in memory of Henry Ames, Semon Amzalak, and Dan Amzalak; the LGBT Fund of Greater Rochester; and contributions from many individuals nationwide. See Colophon on page 104 for special individual acknowledgments.

Cover Design: Daphne Morrissey
Cover Art: "Fruit Hands" by Justine Kelley
Interior Design and Composition: Richard Foerster
BOA Logo: Mirko

BOA Editions books are available electronically through BookShare, an online distributor offering Large-Print, Braille, Multimedia Audio Book, and Dyslexic formats, as well as through e-readers that feature text to speech capabilities.

Library of Congress Cataloging-in-Publication Data

Names: Quintos, Danni, author. | Nezhukumatathil, Aimee, author of foreword.
Title: Two brown dots / poems by Danni Quintos ; foreword by Aimee Nezhukumatathil.
Description: Rochester, NY : BOA Editions, Ltd., 2022. | Series: A. Poulin, Jr. new poets of America series ; 46 | Summary: "Danni Quintos' Poulin Prize-winning debut poetry collection explores what it means to be a mixed-race, multiethnic Asian American girl in Kentucky"— Provided by publisher.
Identifiers: LCCN 2021042486 (print) | LCCN 2021042487 (ebook) | ISBN 9781950774517 (paperback) | ISBN 9781950774524 (ebook)
Subjects: LCGFT: Poetry.
Classification: LCC PS3617.U5898 T88 2022 (print) | LCC PS3617.U5898 (ebook) | DDC 811/.6—dc23/eng/20211018
LC record available at https://lccn.loc.gov/2021042486
LC ebook record available at https://lccn.loc.gov/2021042487

BOA Editions, Ltd.
250 North Goodman Street, Suite 306
Rochester, NY 14607
www.boaeditions.org
A. Poulin, Jr., Founder (1938–1996)

for my Mima, and for Shelli

Contents

III. FOLKLORE

Danni Quintos knows how to create light. After so much darkness brought about by climate change, political strife, and, most recently, a global pandemic among other devastations, I'm so glad for this spark. I'm reminded of that old Rumi missive: "If light is in your heart, you will find your way home." Quintos is a lighthouse when it comes to revealing essential truths about finding your way when you feel alone or misunderstood—our ability to feel lonesome can be just as equaled by our ability to find love, even in the most unexpected ways. This debut thrillingly gives us a triumphant vocabulary with which to make sense, celebrate, and ponder the wild and ecstatic bafflements of coming-of-age, and what it means to insist and cultivate a home for yourself (and others) with courage and grace.

Right away in the first poem, "Portrait of My Dad Through a Tent Window," she writes: "We kept the tent's window unzipped, a gray screen crawling with coppery beetles. The train's wail lulled us asleep & we could see just beyond their bodies: Dad in the yellow-lit kitchen window, watching the lights jump around the tent." We see the luster off the strange beetles, glinting in the night, the haunting sounds of a train, and even the once familiar house and backyard take on a new mysterious glow: a young girl noticing her dad watching out for her and her sister, hoping (perhaps with relief) that the lights "jump[ing] around the tent" might mean his girls are safe, are having fun, that they are close at hand should any harm befall them.

Take her poem "Age Eleven," when a very different kind of knowing that the speaker is being watched electrifies and confounds her, ". . . these boys / have been hiding in the air vents / . . . watching us / slip bras off . . . / They elbow each other / out of the way for the best view, / their faces striped with light, / obsessed as we are." Here girls thrill over being seen, even as the very thought scares them into wants and desires they aren't quite sure they should have yet.

And later in "Youth Group": ". . . I cried // in front of new friends, thought the God-part of my brain/ alive and sparkling." For the speaker in these poems, being struck with light means feeling understood, feeling seen. It's very telling that the speaker knows (and remembers) that initial feeling of sheltering with her sister in the tent, that sensation of which she will return for the rest of the book. She holds that moment up to compare for the rest of her days, even when she becomes a mother and worries over what the future may bring.

Quintos goes on to wrestle with voices and inventions that reveal, in image after image, an extraordinary and captivating foray into motherhood that ends in a stunning suite of epistolary poems addressed to the ironically maternal "Iron Butterfly" of the Philippines herself, former First Lady (and felon), Imelda Marcos.

With a powerful curiosity and beautifully rendered awareness, Quintos' *Two Brown Dots* ends with a whirl of folklore, holding a lantern up to the sometimes difficult questions we are forced to endure in a country that doesn't always know how to receive brown skin. How to receive brown skin that holds desires not often seized upon and selected for a more thoughtful look in American literature. How to receive brown skin that knows "how to kill a chicken . . . in slow taps, how we let the neck bleed into rice." How to receive brown skin "in the TV's glass where their blanched / & smiling ovals once shone."

But here she is, poetry world—refreshingly tenacious, bearing spells and gifts that feel like an everlasting candle through sunrise, through sunset—to guide us in all of our days.

And thank goodness for that.

—Aimee Nezhukumatathil

I.

GIRLHOOD

Portrait of My Dad Through a Tent Window

Ramirez was on the loose. First name Angel & the news made him a monster. A cop in my driveway asking Dad if he'd seen this man, but maybe switching his glance back & forth from the photo to make sure my brown dad with long hair wasn't him. Before we knew about this train-hopping killer, Dad bought us a tent with two rooms & planted it in the backyard. Shelli & I cracked Sprite cans open & Dad washed dark red cherries & put them in a bowl for us. Our flashlights made hand shadows into geese & talking dogs, made our ghost story faces monstrous, light shining up our noses. We kept the tent's window unzipped, a gray screen crawling with coppery beetles. The train's wail lulled us asleep & we could see just beyond their bodies: Dad in the yellow-lit kitchen window, watching the lights jump around the tent.

UNBREAK MY HEART

For my eleventh
birthday, Jo sent me
a blue striped
turtleneck, a burgundy
velvet T-shirt, & matte,
brick lipstick
that made me feel
so grown up
in the mirror.
This was after
Mom moved out
& the house
became Dad's,
after Dad
let Toni Braxton's
Unbreak My Heart
play & play
on the kitchen
radio while he
washed dishes
& cooked Cajun
catfish fillets,
he showed us
photos of Jo
& her daughter,
Natasha.
Jo, laughing
with wavy hair
falling over one
side of her face.
Jo, looking serious,
straight into

the camera's eye
& Natasha,
three years old,
riding a Big Wheel
over shaggy, beige
carpet. Jo's
screen name
was EUROJO
& she asked me
about what I liked
to write & draw,
the names of my best
friends & enemies.
Soon, Dad was driving
his little red car
north to Maryland,
the windows down
& wind tangling
my hair with my sister's.
Jo & Natasha
lived in an apartment
above storage units:
big orange doors
& Jo answering
the phone
Fort Knox Storage?
in her English accent.
There, my sister & I
snuck under
the half-shut doors
of empty units,
swatted mosquitoes
that circled our ears,
played hide & seek
with Natasha who wore

a party dress
& tights scuffed
at the knees.
I thought I had a new
little sister,
I thought Dad was happy
with Jo, the spoonful
of Nutella
in the kitchen,
the hands that taught me
how to knit
yarn into cloth,
the woman who
told me she had certain
colors that made her
coppery blonde hair
pop: aqua, amethyst,
moss. My last
memory of her
is in her yard, where
she smiles
under my dad's arm.
Her neighbors ask
if she will move
to our Kentucky home
& she answers
Yes. Yes, but
her boxes never arrive.
The phone doesn't
ring with her voice
on the line. I imagine
she forgets us.

ON BEING ASKED TO REPRESENT YOUR COUNTRY

Our elementary school called itself a global
studies school. A whole neighborhood
      of international kids in our district

took a bus I once heard a friend call, *The Oriental
Bus* & when I got mad, I couldn't explain why.
      I knew those kids were different, but

didn't I see myself in them? A girl named Ninda
from Indonesia who everyone thought was my sister.
      Twin! I called her, 'til she told me to stop.

Every time we had geography reports I got
the Philippines. Did I choose this every time?
      The first two, probably—but the third

felt like a trap, like I'd be regurgitating the same
facts about Spanish colonization & rice agriculture
      forever. & then there was the National Anthem:

the music teacher searched last names on her rosters
for all the most diverse fifth graders. She asked us
      to dress in the costumes of our countries & sing

at the local hockey game. We weren't good singers
& I didn't know what Filipinos wore. Even my lola
      just said, *T-shirt & jeans, what you're wearing now.*

My mom's pink kimono had ink stains on the obi
from waiting tables, so I had to borrow Ayumi Okuda's
      dad's kimono, a foot too long.

I felt both proud & dumb, letting it drag
behind me on the scratched ice where we sang
out of tune & in our parents' clothes.

When Clothes Make You Cousins

Kendra Worthington was the new kid in second grade
& we were fast friends—both at Crestwood Daycare

after school, both in the yellow dots
reading group with third graders, which made us feel

smarter & better. She transferred from Booker T.
where almost everyone was Black or brown

& she told me their library had a system
with paddle placeholders, so when you took

a book from the shelf you knew where it went.
Kendra had this jacket, acid wash denim, lined

with fleece. I don't remember how we got there,
but its label said it was made in the Philippines. This meant

we were related—cousins. In big tennis courts
on the playground we played hot lava & laughed

We're cousins! we told our friends, the proof on a tag
at the nape of her neck.

Scary Spice

She was in my fourth-grade class, shy
& curly-headed, her face red with crying
that first day, her mom steering her shoulders
to the coat closet. Her seat was next to mine,

our names laminated & taped down. I asked
which Spice Girl she would be. I always wanted
to be Ginger, but got bullied into being Scary
since I was the only brown girl playing. At recess,

she started telling stories about how much
she was from Kentucky, unlike me. Great-great
grandparents all buried in this town & where
were mine? *My family was friends with Henry Clay*

loud enough for everyone on the bus to hear
after a field trip to Ashland estate. We'd seen
hair-sprayed raspberry pastries in the kitchen,
set up to look like the Clays were on their way

downstairs. The smoke house, the slaves' quarters,
the elaborate garden, a wall of hedges.
My grandpa played on the UK basketball team
coached by Adolph Rupp, she bragged in the car

as we passed Rupp Arena. I didn't have brags
like this. Didn't even know my dad's dad's name.
All I knew that got passed down was from the summer
we flew to the Philippines when I was six.

My lola showed me how to kill a chicken
with a hatchet, knocking the blade against its wound
in slow taps, how we let the neck bleed into rice.

CRUSH SPELL BY A FIFTH-GRADE WITCH

It's always Duke Prather.
I used to make deals

with myself, if I hold on
to this rope & don't fall

off my skis, I'll get to kiss
Duke Prather. If I can walk

home in less than 50 steps
I will marry Duke Prather.

All the MASH games where
he got crossed off my list, soda

tabs I tore off the can at D or P.
I wanted the kickball

to leave my foot & shoot
straight into his arms. Sunday

mass, I chose to sit three pews
behind his family. If he wears

his embroidered belt & khaki shorts,
if his mother shushes his sisters,

if he crosses himself after the wafer
it means we're meant to be.

Cross Your Forehead, Mouth, & Heart

It was a hard pew & gold page book, every word
planned & printed on a Sunday future. Voices & organs
echoing into bored tall space. It was a dress I hated

to wear & wondering what the wafer tasted like, if it was
sweet. It was pretending I had the Apostle's Creed memorized
& shame that I didn't know the moves yet: sit, stand, kneel, cross

your forehead, mouth, & heart with your thumb. It was not
knowing who I was supposed to pray to or what. How I asked
God to say hello to my kindergarten teacher & goldfish, but then

what should I say after? I confessed sins in a wooden phone booth
without a phone. Sour wine on my tongue. A girl's veil on fire
in front of me. Altar boys in long robes with Adidas sneakers

underneath. The robot drone of tired adults reciting a prayer,
the baskets on long sticks reaching down the aisle, the dollar
my lola gave me to toss in. The coloring book of apostles & doves

I left blank. How my clicking heels in C.C.D. Sunday school
got me in trouble; the questions too, asking if Moses went to heaven
or what Jesus's middle name was & did he have pets? The telephone

game that made us blaspheme: *Jesus was a hotdog*. The powdered
donuts & hot chocolate in the fellowship hall after mass. How
my lola made a collage for the confirmation I skipped, pretending

it was me: magazine grapes & catechism, my name in gold letters.
The year I told my lola I didn't want to go to C.C.D. anymore
because the only other Filipina girl in the class moved to Florida,

because I was the last brown girl in class asking why Jesus
is so pale. But the real reason was the trouble, the time I was made
to stand alone for the rest of class, keep my shoes & mouth quiet.

AGE ELEVEN

A creaky foldout
sofa with copper
flowers at Mom's new
old house is the new
old bed I share
with my sleeping
sister while our pet
hedgehog runs away,
and for months
she scratches
in the walls, survives
on crickets
& roly-polies, until
she returns, lured
by peanut butter
in a cage trap, metal
door snapped shut
while I am belly-down
in a closet clubhouse,
flashlight-reading
the CD booklet
to *Jagged Little Pill*,
memorizing lyrics like
I'm brave but
I'm chicken shit,
like *Would she go*
down on you in
a theatre? I don't know
what these words mean,
but the feeling
of reading cuss words
in the dark & the nettled

burn of Alanis's voice
gives me some kind
of power, & Mom lets
me sing these cusses,
so long as I promise
only at home where
it's safe. At school
I'm the girl wearing weird
outfits: a blue daisy
minidress over jeans
& everyone talks
about me behind
their palms, a girl with
blonde, straight hair
asks me where I got it,
smiling mean right
into my face, & when I
dress up like Michael Jackson
for a group project
about the 80s: one sparkly
glove & piecey hair pulled
back in a ponytail, crotch
-grabbing myself & high-pitch
voice, I don't break
character. I am shameless,
the funny girl who didn't
get invited to Courtney's
freakdancing party, but
I do sleep over
at my best friend's, where
we empty her caboodle
of eye shadows & pencils
on her bed, smear colors
on our eyes, practicing
for middle school. I make her

watch the *Dirty Dancing*
tape I snuck in my pillowcase
& tell her they do it
three times, & with
the volume down, we see how
Baby gets put in a corner,
and Patrick Swayze
glazed with sweat
& lake water, twisting
his shiny muscles to the music.
She'll tell her mom
the next morning
at breakfast, crying,
she'll say they did it
three times. We play
the game we call *what if*
while we fall asleep,
whispering into
each other's hair, What if
Duke Prather asked you
to prom & gave you
his letterman's jacket?
Everything that happened
to the twins in Sweet Valley,
we want to happen
to us. What if Jack Ulrich
gave you a flower unlike any
other in the world? Picture
the rose from *Beauty & the Beast*,
withering under a glass dome.
We imagine these boys
have been hiding in the air vents
the whole time, watching us
slip bras off our boyish chests.
They elbow each other

out of the way for the best view,
their faces striped with light,
obsessed as we are.

LETTER TO MY CHILDHOOD CRUSH

after Tia Clark

Dear Duke,

Stop doing karate & flexing your tiny bicep on the playground, stop buzzing your hair & leaving your bangs long, stop wearing soccer cleats & tube socks

to school, stop looking through me like you can see the field behind me. Stop telling your little sisters to pinch me as hard as they can with the sharp corners

of their nails. Stop smiling at Amelia. Stop making that dimple appear on your left cheek, stop pretending you didn't get the pink letter I kissed & sent you

after I looked up your address in the phone book. Stop pushing your forearm to mine on the playground, saying *a brownskin can't marry a whiteskin.*

I am the kickball here. I am over the hedges, out of bounds, & you with arms above your head, run the bases, triumphant.

THE RULES

Jennifer isn't allowed to like Francisco even though
he's in love with her: always follows her during recess,

calls her name with a soft Y sound at the beginning.
Don't you think he's cute? I ask. *No!* she says

like someone is listening in, someone like her dad.
Francisco is brown as me and from Brazil.

He has an accent and beautiful smile. He draws
hearts with Jennifer's name in the middle.

Jennifer isn't allowed to play with me or Tommy,
whose dad is Black and died when we were in first grade.

I remember when they called him out of class to tell him
and he didn't come back for weeks.

You and Tommy look dirty, she says, repeating
what her dad tells her. Jennifer is allowed to play

with Yolie and have her sleep over and everything,
even though Yolie is from Cuba and has a strong accent

and I grew up here and have no accent. It's because
Yolie is pale as Jennifer and Cara and our teacher

Mrs. E. Smith. It's because Jennifer's dad
doesn't think Yolie looks dirty.

BROWN GIRLS

The summer after Mom moved out
& into the Oldham Avenue house, we played

in all the front yards like they were ours.
Flashlight tag & clapping lightning bugs

dead in our hands for that toxic glow.
Then, that Ratliff boy across the street

asked if I was one of those orphans from TV.
Before that, I thought we were all the same

kids, same-sized houses, same bus to school.
Suddenly, we were brown & they weren't. I let out

a sharp vowel & stomped back to our front
door between the hedges, into the house

where our dark-skinned dad never showed,
the house where Mom moved—to be with

her pale, bearded boyfriend. But that kid's voice
at my back, still asking his dumb question

in the streetlights. It kept ringing in the dark
like cicadas, little voice outside our window

Well, is she? bruising me in ways I didn't yet
understand. And every summer after, a whirring

reminder that I didn't belong here, a little song
sung at me by the bodies that slept for years

underground. How we couldn't see what he saw:
two brown girls under a white couple's roof.

Sixth-Grade Invisibility Studies

Somehow my new blue jean flares
became high-waters & everyone could see
my babyish purple socks. My glasses got crooked
on my face, my hips spread wide & I started
to bleed through my pants unpredictably.

This is when I tried to erase myself, pushed
my limp hair in front of my eyes to become
invisible. A boy in art class called me the N-word
& smiled. I wanted to disappear & steal his backpack,
dump it out the window, math book & pencils spilling

in the courtyard where only birds could get in.
In orchestra class, my bow sawed the wrong way
during the moonlight sonata, my notes
too flat or too sharp. The teacher made me

play alone: imagine a violin floating in the air,
squeaking. I got caught passing a note in Social Studies,
triangle folded & flicked across a table, I was made
an example of, a 500-word essay that no one wanted

to write. I ran slowest in gym class, little legs pumping,
a full lap behind the athletic older girls who took the tights
from my locker & tied them in a knot like a flag

up high. I pretended it wasn't my locker, pressed my back
against the metal gills & tried not to breathe. All the eyes
watching the empty legs waving in imaginary wind. I waited

for everyone to change back into their Old Navy shirts
& Gap jeans, gather their hair into ponytails & leave.

The bell rang in the empty locker room, I untied the knot
& slipped my invisible feet in, like a jellyfish's translucent

& stinging tentacles, like its empty

head, a plastic bag.

Who I Wanted to Be Instead

My favorite shirt used to be
a polyester button-up
that looked like a wet oil painting
of a rainbow, stirred in circles.
I wore it to feel cool until
a North Carolina beach trip
with my older cousin
showed me what a baby
I was. She wore thin
camisoles with lace around
the cleavage, jeans so tight
they creaked when she bent
over & here I was, Professor
Psychedelic, eleven years old
still trying to figure out
how to wear eyeliner.
We walked to Walmart
& bought *Something*
About Mary & after watching
it in the nighttime basement,
I wished I could just be
like my cousin, smoking secret
cigarettes with gangly boys
under the dock, or like Cameron Diaz:
so cool she could swipe
cum in her hair & look cute,
so cute men did long-cons
for her affection. I blew out
candles for years, wishing
to be like her, blonde & braless,
everyone smiling, pining
for my attention.

Unpretty

It was a sleepover & she'd never put her hair up
in a high ponytail before. We'd bought cheap
necklaces that split hearts into even best friend pieces,

but tonight we were all sick of her: how she thought
the lyrics to TLC's "Unpretty" were *Damn!*
I'm pretty! how she cried mascara-blue tears

because if we got redistricted, she'd have to
break up with her boyfriend & now
we were all talking seriously about which song

to make a dance routine to & where was she?
Her face almost touching the mirror, never breaking
self-eye-contact & bobbing her head

to make the high ponytail bounce. She didn't care
about the dance. Instead, she made us go around
the room & say what we didn't like about ourselves.

We were all eleven, a never-ending list of the awkward
ways our bodies were changing. We wished
our boobs were real boobs & not these nubs, wished

we were taller, skinnier, had our periods, had hair
in the right places, had a smaller nose, bigger
eyes, lighter hair, the right clothes, the right makeup.

Her response was always, *TRUE!* blurted
without looking up from her Teen People.
In a few years a rumor spread about her, so gross

it would have to be at least part true. Something
about a boy fingering her on a playground,
hitting the wrong button & she pooped in his hand.

But didn't we all grin when we heard? Were we
the engine behind this story, embellishing
as we passed it on: the floral skirt she dirtied, the smear

on the slide, & never the boy whose hand misfired.
& didn't we all want to believe it? Our own
bodies were safe & hidden in our clothes.

Boobs

after Ellen Hagan

In fifth-grade gym class I ran into the padded walls
and felt like marbles bruised me under my shirt. That night

I dreamt they were big & flouncy and I looked at myself
in a mirror, laughing. In a field at recess I did a cartwheel

and Elliott Fess saw my shirt fly up to my chin. I'd forgotten
we were different now. When I asked, did you see anything?

he said, just two brown dots. I wanted him to feel embarrassed
or changed by the sight of me. Or maybe to see me as a girl, a body.

In high school I was crazy for my boyfriend who never tried
to push his palm to my bra, even an accidental thumb didn't

graze me. I wondered if there was something wrong with them:
the shape, the size, did I wear the wrong bra? He guilt-prayed

for forgiveness during youth group worship with his palms
raised to the ceiling, trying to erase those afternoons of just kissing

& nothing else but friction: our bodies trying to get loose
from their husks, out of breath with all our clothes on, his mother

down the hall, and Jesus watching the whole time. A couple years later,
his best friend was the first boy to touch any part of me, to peel

my clothes from me & see more than just two brown dots. A secret
we kept in our breast pockets, the ways our bodies betrayed us.

WHAT GIRLS LEARN

the coolest girl of the playground was either
emily b., whose straight blonde hair sometimes

fell across her perfect blue eyes, or amelia h.,
who grew armpit hair before any of us. she showed off

her wispy new underbrush or maybe we all snuck looks
as she crossed the monkey bars with her arms up. the weirdo

of the playground was sometimes caity c., who'd hold
her crotch while playing outfield because, she said, it felt good.

and sometimes it was the creep of the playground, mandy s.,
who'd chase us around the wooden castle with a wide-eyed grin,

waving her middle finger in the air, threatening to push it up our butts
& shouting *c'mere!* she was the friend who knew all the dirty jokes & sex

stories she'd tell in a treehouse, or standing in the lunch line
or far away in the field where adults couldn't hear. one about a little boy

named deeper having sex with a teacher. the *inside her* part had me
picturing a tiny boy in a cave, hollering out. still, they made me feel

like someone put their finger in my bellybutton, like I had to pee.
mandy was really into cyber sex, especially during sleepovers.

a computer in the basement where we typed all the dirty knowledge
in our heads & clicked send, never picturing the hands that typed back.

our focus was making it believable, making them think we knew
the ways our bodies could open. we typed eat you out. pussy. butthole.

we learned to say 17/f, blonde & tall, learned to lie &
be what they wanted.

THE WORST PART OF RIDING THE BUS

In sixth grade
a girl on our bus
was murdered.
After her body
was found in the park
by a little boy looking
for his ball, we all said
nice things about her,
pretended she was
the nicest girl
on the bus, our best friend.
Before that, she was missing.
Last seen on her bike
according to
announcements,
but those who knew her
knew she was last seen
giving her mother
the finger,
last seen poking me
in the back
on the bus, last seen:
her face covered
in pink pimples,
her teeth sharp as an angry
dog's, her little sister
rolling her eyes & screaming
I'ma tell mom!
Last seen flirting
with my first boyfriend
& asking me if I was
Mexican & illegal.

When her curly
blonde & snarling head
didn't appear
on the school bus steps,
we sighed
letting all the balloons
in our lungs go.

Mispronunciation

Always a *yell* after my name on the first
day of school & a soft squishy Q—*Qwin-toes*.
Correcting the first name always stuck
but the Q never hardened to a sharp point.

Sometimes in Spanish class I'd become
Keen-toss & the roll-caller would beam
at their ability to read a different language.
On the baby tape my mom made when I was two

I am mouthing the mic too close, saying my name
lazy: *Ken-toes*. I had a boyfriend in high school
who, for our three years together, mispronounced me:
always Quinn at the beginning like an overripe

cantaloupe, a forgotten jack-o'-lantern whose head
caves in to a waxy pulp. I want the K-sound to cut
like a chef's knife, my kin evoked from the past
& Kentucky claiming me as one of its own.

THE MIX CD I MADE WHEN I WAS SIXTEEN

1. bathwater (no doubt)   white pickup truck with grey bucket seats

2. wonderwall (oasis)   a window i had to crank down

3. heartbreaker (led zeppelin)   the shifter in his palm

4. honey pie (the beatles)   orange elvis glasses on the dash

5. teenage dirtbag (wheatus)   balled-up gym socks behind the seat

6. say it ain't so (weezer)   a copy of siddhartha he borrowed & never read

7. when it hurts so bad (lauryn hill)   its cover, triangle-folded face down

8. creep (radiohead)   armrest full of burned cds with some girl's scribble

9. sleep to dream (fiona apple)   chapsticks on the floor rolling

10. ex-factor (lauryn hill)   every time we'd brake. his ugly flip-flopped feet

11. heartbreaker (mariah carey)   pushing clutch & gas, the flutter & cough

12. on & on (erykah badu)   an engine giving up

YOUTH GROUP

Later in high school it was me saying no
to youth group invitations from my boyfriend
who hid his heathen erections & stained

sheets from his mother. The boy who knew
if he could save my soul, I would stop trying
to taste his tongue & put lips on the hair below

his bellybutton. How many nights did he pray to calm
the sex-crazed demon inside me, keep my bitten
-nail fingers off the zipper of his corduroys. I came

around, finally, went to Sunday night rock bands
for Jesus & Wednesday night bible study. I watched
passionate, goateed 30-somethings sweat

under spotlights & pray out loud like God
was a bro they could put on speakerphone. Maybe
part of it was the time I wanted to spend

with that boy. Like his love of Christ would transfer
& he'd be allowed to love me too. His parents
might stop saying he needed a *saved girl*. So, I stopped

rolling my eyes & started believing, the lyrics
about a lamb filled my mouth, my hands warmed
by a girl next to me who believed, too, that I was good.

I hoped the holy water splashed on my infant head
in '87 was enough to save me. I held sweaty hands
& read verses, memorized, copied down in curly cursive,

underlined in pen, asked questions like, *Is it sacrilegious
to read the bible while listening to Led Zeppelin?* I joined
a small group & had an accountability partner, I cried

in front of new friends, thought the God-part of my brain
alive & sparkling. I prayed every night & out loud
with strangers, ladled soup into homeless bowls & sang

the songs like I meant them. I meant it. Even after
the boyfriend broke up with me because we couldn't
stop tearing into each other, but really because

there was another girl with long eyelashes
called Julie or Hannah whose lips he wanted to taste.
Even after that I went to Costa Rica on a mission trip,

ate black beans & fish, scrambled eggs for breakfast
in a dirt floor house, remembered not to flush toilet paper
& washed the host-family's dishes in their rot-filled

concrete sink. I prayed & praised in Spanish, painted
a cemetery wall that didn't need painting, taught little girls
words in English when they hadn't asked. The boys moved

stones from a pile to a ditch, sweating dirty for the Lord
& thinking they made a difference. I thought
I was chosen, called to missions: teaching & spreading

God's word—helping the poor by being poor & brown
with them. Me: the brown girl in a pale, Kentucky sea.
I thought my skin color a gift, while the other youths

would return to their big subdivision McMansions
to eat strawberries in December, hardly changed & never
able to blend & belong somewhere else, the way I could.

ODE TO COUNTRY DIPS

It starts with a fat J & a playlist / a car full & all the windows down. / Take a right on Military Pike / where the traffic lights & rules start to disappear. / The roads narrow & undulate & all our stomachs flip / while we breathe smoke like teenage dragons / who love Missy Elliott & Peaches. / Daryl drives 80 & the trees blur. / Caity makes us stop & smell the country air / says, hear that? about the cicadas whirring. / We watch heat lightning clamor against clouds. / We pass tobacco barns / printed black & gray on color film. / The horse fences are music staffs / guiding us to a crescendo. / There's a road called Frogtown Lane / & in the dark we swing a sharp left. / The hedges grow around us until a clearing. / The bodies of rusted old cars & school buses, / the ghosts of girls once on dips before us, / red-eyed & smoke full & lungs blaring lyrics. / We reverse to escape & find ourselves / giddy with relief / & in the stories / we come off braver & bolder / than we appeared.

EIGHTEEN

& no one expects you to be anywhere
or do anything. 800 dollars of graduation
money fills your pockets & you lie
in thank you notes, you don't mention
how many boxes of camel lights you'll buy
or how you'll slip their cellophanes down
& drop a ten-dollar marble of weed, fold
the corners & burn the edge for a seal.
You buy gas too, to fill your car & drive
north to Ft. Thomas, go to parties
with new boys that haven't heard
of your heartbreak, they only care
about the lips on your face, the tongue
in your mouth, or if you'll lift your hips
to slip your shorts off under blankets
when you share their beds.

II.

MOTHERHOOD

TRYING

O pink watercolor spot
in my panties, O thermometer's dip
in the morning, O cramps
Oh, cramps! crawling up
my uterus like weak & nagging
claws, O disappointment,
O single pink line on a stick
after three long minutes,
O pineapple & ginger, oval
brown vitamin in my throat,
O fake yoga with my hips
in the air, O good sex
& real good sex & ok sex,
O cervix, firm & low
O egg white consistency,
O two week wait & more
pineapple, O leafy greens
& unpacked bowl, O elliptical
machine, water bottle sloshing,
O hopeful mother-in-law,
O sad tampon, O bottle
of wine, O calendar

LUTEAL PHASE ENDS

At least my body is making
progress, the days between
ovulation & menstruation

enough for something, maybe.
Today I woke with the pain
I'm used to—slow ache

in the night while red honey
leaks from me. I am not
too sad, I buy myself dry

hopped cider, a sour ale, a pint
of chocolate peanut butter
ice cream & a diva cup.

I buy myself new nail polish.
I am 30, no more *just* in front
of my age, I am in this body.

I darken my eyebrows
with pencil & test the texture
of my cervix in the shower

like a deeply hidden pulse.
What else can I do but try
& keep this body satisfied.

The Eighth Month

1. *Hurry & Rage*

All I want to hurry is this ocean
inside me. The salt's tide churning
in my sleep. When I'm still
he's moving: surf-swimming, somersault
under my ribs. I want to bring
him out to the air, this fish-child
with sealed lids, see him squirm & punch
the cold. For now, I am his taxi—
yellow checkered dress draping
over the beach-ball shape of me.
All road rage & middle fingers
for anyone who crosses me.

2. *Dreams*

I keep dreaming I'm at a job
I don't have anymore: food service
& grumpy customers, a simple task
that won't get done, then a sharp
push on my bladder & I'm awake,
headed for the bathroom again, hoping
the paper is hanging down
so I don't have to search for its end
in the dark, in all this heavy breathing.
I heave myself off couches & up
stairs, trying to hold in the hot air
balloon always waiting to expel. Things
could be worse, I know & keep
remembering how ordinary

all of this is—every kid I see at work
had a mother who was probably
this pregnant at some point, who did
that impossible animal thing
of pushing them out.

3. *Other People's Birth Stories*

My lola's midwife sister kept her
from eating too much—
always a big bowl of broth
before every meal. And something
about her appetite was broken too—
her new husband like a ghost
from a dream, leaving
her big & carrying someone
who looked so much like him.
She says the baby didn't turn
until a few days before labor began
& it was so easy. No urgency
or panic, just a slick, round baby
moving from inside to outside world.
She tells the story more than 50 years
later, the memory of soreness gone.
Ache, loss, joy, loneliness: gone.
What she does remember: that she could
do it all over again the next day
& why do women even complain?

4. *Carrying*

Sometimes I feel trapped in this body
when I have an itch on my spine & wonder

how I can reach around myself to scratch.
This pendulous surface:

        like a heavy box of dishes
        like an anvil in a package
        like a sleeping kettlebell
    I cannot take off. In the night I sometimes
roll over, forgetting the body I've become & it pulls
me. Some late hours I'm full of pee & have to
carry myself off the bed for relief, grunting
with each cold, heavy step.

First Milk

After all that birth, the legs you've used your whole life
are now wobbly & the lake where your son used to swim

trickles from between them. The spaces between your fingers
feel sticky. The first thing the baby does is search for the warmth

of you, his face a small suction cup for the mounds you've been
building. Those first golden drops, thick as honey, spill from you

& the nurse rushes to catch them with a plastic spoon. God forbid
they soak your hospital gown or run down your rib cage. Once, you were

a girl with two breasts like the smallest constellation, an incomplete ellipsis.
Today, they find new purpose. Today they are nourishment & comfort,

food, water, some kind of magic. They work so hard after years
of thinking themselves merely decorative.

Breastfeeding

To begin I was just a girl:
wet clay sculpted

right, perfect shape
for his mouth: sharp

little gums, hungry
tongue. After I was always

ready—erasers, gum drops,
fingertips. & mornings I am

a cement sculpture of myself:
skin taut & often leaking.

I am the paper grocery bag
whose wet stain grows

in the shape of an unknown
country. I depend

on machinery now:
the rhythmic pump

whose voice chants
whose plastic horn fills

drop by drop, I collect
for the hours I am away.

Yes, worth it. Yes, proud
of every thigh roll's deep crevice

of cheeks like ripe plums.
& even if I am deflated

like an old birthday balloon
these breasts are full

of purpose. Oh body, how
you keep on making.

Breast Lump

Praise the nurse's hands that held mine
wearing blue latex gloves while a needle

shoved into my numb & unsuspecting
breast. Praise the midwife's hand too

searching for this marble I've carried
in my chest nearly a decade. Praise her belief

that it wasn't right, her caution, her call
the afternoon to check on me after

the biopsy. Praise too my grandmother's
missing breast. The one replaced by

an intersection scar, her many biopsies,
her casual dismissal of mine while she lay

in a hospital bed, tubes in her arm, true
crime on TV. Praise the man I love

& sleep next to, whose sleep was scarce
in his worry. 1:00 a.m. & it was morning to him,

hands in soil, planting tomatoes, trying
to not think too hard about the breast

that feeds his son, that meets his palm
so certainly. & praise again the hands

of nurses pushing against me, pressure
to the glued wound while I cried

on the table, trying to understand my limits:
how I cannot lift my one-year-old

for a few days & the weight of not knowing
what this knot in me means.

Naptime Haibun

We had to make a reservation to hike. Lots of masks, lots of kids, lots of poison ivy right off the path. Mud & roots lead the way, big sticky puddles with boot prints. *This one is a hoof!* We drink water, practice running & climbing, hear a creek, spot a butterfly. Gus says, *Get me down!* when he's tired of riding in the backpack. I point out thorny berry bushes and a huge dead millipede, whose orange legs look like fringe. There's an apple waiting for each of us in the car. There's a windows-down breeze & horses to point at, there's a yellow field of flowers. When we get home, we have to make deals: if you go in now, we can come out later. If you wash your hands, we can eat our lunch. Time out for throwing an apple down the hallway. I drive Gus around the neighborhood & transfer him from car seat to shoulder to bed.

O holy naptime,
I don't want to imagine
routine without you.

Breast Pain

In pandemic June I find an egg
        -sized lump, angry & hot, under

my shirt. A toddler's hug makes
        me wince. I wear a mask, a cotton pink

gown. I awkwardly hug a machine
        as it bites each breast with mechanical

x-ray teeth. I have always been scared
        of these breasts. Mine formed painfully

as glass marbles under my skin. A bruise
        & bloom, the year my lola had hers

excised: perpendicular scar like an intersection
        across her. A special bra, one nipple

in the mirror under her church blouse. My breasts
        inherited thick, ropey tissue; a risk from her

side, a rust-colored rosary worn from prayer.

Pandemic Fall Haibun

I read part of an essay & unravel part of a sweater I'm making. I gather pawpaws from the front yard with Gus. Cut around the equator & scoop out seeds. Berries, pancakes, put your shoes on. I call my lola to ask how her arm is. Hurts all the time & she wants to go home. We go to Meg's where Gus & Jo play horses & dinosaurs. *Pretend you're a velociraptor & I'm your baby.* Robo-dogs, a bow & arrow. I am mosquito-bit by the pool, then consoling a crying Gus, out the door—buckle up, take your blanket. Gus falls asleep & I peel him from the car seat. I keep quiet & read old poems, heat up lunch. I think of Monday & what waits for me: thermometer, computers draped with caution tape, the foreheads & eyes of all my students, their imagined noses & chins.

In-person classes,
lola in the hospital;
first pandemic fall.

Something from Nothing

It feels like we're doing everything
in preparation for instead of

to distract ourselves from
pregnancy. Yes, I wish I was

nauseous & constipated, I wish my ankles
would swell, my feet wide as skis.

Zach is planting & cultivating
all the space we have outside:

greens, fruit trees, root vegetables,
climbing peas & herbs whose leaves

take lacy doily shape. I am turning
long lines of wool into cloth: knots

knitting with bamboo needles while I watch
everything my TV suggests. This is self

-reliance. Reproduction & production,
something growing where there didn't

before seem to be space.

Letters to Imelda Marcos

I.
Dear Imelda,

Everyone cares about your shoes so much
that they forget everything else, & I don't
mean they forget your extravagant dresses
& scarves, or the way you glisten with Cartier

diamonds. They forget, or never knew at all,
all the ways you failed, you monstered, how
many Ferragamo pumps you bought when
your people went barefoot, how you stole

everything & made it yours: palace, power,
years from the people you imprisoned.
Imelda, you're always trying to distract us
with a shining thing, the thousands

of crystals sewn to your once-worn gown,
no mention of the women gone blind
for them, their fingers cramped & crooked.
You are surrounded by Filipinos who tell you

Yes & praise you for your beauty & genius & I
am not one of them. I am fixated on your ugly,
your misdirection, the stories you repeat
to paint yourself as mother—diamonds & diapers

in your bag during panicked exit. You want
everyone to say, how beautiful, how kind.

II.
Dear Imelda,

Your mother & my grandmother
share a narrative too—

My lola was born in 1939, the year
after your mother died.

They are both Remedios, named
for the Virgin of Remedies.

They are both from Baliwag,
Bulacan, a small town of rice fields

& carabao, baskets, pandesal,
salty small fish & tamarind

vines growing along creeks.
Your Remedios slept on a table

in your father's garage, where your
sister was conceived. What a scandal

in Baliwag, like my pregnant
lola, whose husband left her

alone in the heat of broken tile
floors, frogs singing her asleep.

Both women held their swollen bodies
without remedy, without the men

who were supposed to save them.

III.
Dear Imelda,

Sometimes I see you as that aunt
in trouble, exiled for the ways
she embezzled, but lord, you should
see her count money, the way
her hands move, the flit of the bills
between her fingers. She was the second
wife of an uncle: young, shiny trophy,
mirrors lined the walls so she could smile
at herself. And you, I imagine,
love your reflection too. Silk
shoes, gold necklace, the way
your hair mimics the Philippine Sea
at night: all dark & sparkle. She even
calls herself Imelda, privately, trying
on your extravagance, the swipe
of her Mastercard at Macy's, the weight
of a bracelet she can't afford.

IV.
Dear Imelda,

Here's a story my grandmother tells me: A flood
in Pampanga soaked houses to their tin foreheads
& the US sent dinner rolls to help. Everyone knew

relief was on the way, their food floated in muddy
water. But it was delayed. You, the first lady, decided
to have your workers unwrap & repackage the bread,

mark it: FROM THE FIRST LADY. When it arrived
it was covered with a soft, green fur. Inedible lumps
with your name on them.

V.
Dear Imelda,

My lola's heart is what keeps her from the Philippines,
she says she would be dead before they could drive her
across country roads to a hospital, hours. That ticking timer.

> You once said, *The heart, undoubtedly, is the center of life.*
> You come back to the Philippines after your exile, after hiding
> your beauty queen face from the cameras.

That abused dog, no one knows if it'll sink its teeth into her
ribs again, numb her arm, squeeze the air from her birdbone body.
She showed me an x-ray when her hand was taped down

with tubes. The arteries like swollen rivers, all that water
over the sides. The doctor said no more salt. Salt will stiffen
her veins, grip her brain & squeeze out the words & faces

she used to know. They will fall from her ears, out the corners
of her eyes 'til she forgets everything: the house where she raised
my dad, the acacia tree her father planted in a bright green rice field.

> Your heart unbroken, you return to celebrity: headshots
> autographed & thrown like confetti. Your children run
> for office & win. Your dynasty regenerates at the same rate
>   that Filipinos forget.

III.

FOLKLORE

MILKFISH

if your mother craves milkfish when she's pregnant with you & if
the sea stops putting their gaping mouths on your father's hook, & if
your father begs the sea for more, he will owe the saltwater something. you,
black-haired & seven years old, will be swallowed by a wave. forget
your best friends or the chapter book you haven't finished. forget the freckled
neck of the boy you stare at during english class & sometimes during mass.
forget, too, your mother's warm hands on your shoulders before she braids
your hair into ropes, her ensaymadas sprinkled with cheese & sugar. your feet
won't fit in any pair of sandal or sneaker, you'll feel those bones splay, soft
as straw. maybe you imagine this underwater life as glint & dazzle, scallop shell
bikinis, bottle-nose dolphins, & pearls plentiful as fish eggs. instead,
the seaweed strangles you in sleep, plastic six-pack rings handcuff your wrists,
& all the skeletons of smaller fish tangle in your hair like ugly combs. cola cans
are the only sparkle, twisting their bodies into blades in the sand. when the moon
is a white circle your feet will come back. walk to your old house where
your father disappears into a quiet nothing & find your mother still cooking
milkfish. milkfish: stuffed & baked, fried in oil, pickled in vinegar & garlic,
bodies not unlike your own.

I spilled juice on the plane's seat, stuck my fingers in the armrest ashtray, had to pee at all the wrong times. We flew for a wedding of relatives I'd never met: me in an off-shoulder party dress, throwing petal to path, smile-nodding to no one. My lola wanted me to know the faces of aunts & cousins, their voices, the heavy air, the taste of coconut scraped by a spoon, & even the language I never learned, just its animals & exclamations, its body parts & potluck dishes. I ate mango for the first time, sticky sweet orange-yellow and told my lola, *it's gooder than a peach!* A pig in the backyard gave birth to eleven piglets, wiggle-squealing & the size of puppies, I wanted to bring one back with me. She wanted me to get my ears pierced. *All the other little girls will have theirs pierced, even the babies.* I asked, how much does it hurt? pinched the skin on her arm—this much?

POND'S WHITE BEAUTY

My sister & I watch a commercial:
twin Filipina beauties washing their faces.

They splash water like diamonds, velvety
suds. Black silk hair & smooth, pink apple

cheeks, both paler than any relatives
we've met here, paler than the quiet Welsh

& Japanese blood in both of us. On the screen
a blind date in a blazer rings the doorbell.

The more porcelain sister answers—
her fluorescence lights his stupid smile.

The door opens wider to reveal her
apricot twin: flushed with melanin

next to the sharp, pallid sister. The man frowns.
We frown, knowing that the next scene

will be the sister sharing her secret
potion: Just use Pond's White Beauty

fairness cream to bleach the sun from your
skin, to make you milky translucent.

On the second date, he sees them both
glowing ghostly identical, laughing

at how beautiful they've both become,
unable to tell which girl is his date.

We are two sisters in the middle
of the world where the sun paints us

bronze. In the dark instant between
commercials, our brown faces appear

in the TV's glass where their blanched
& smiling ovals once shone.

SELF-PORTRAIT AS MANANANGGAL

They ask me where I'm from & the answer is hundreds of years old. Is that last name Spanish? From Spain? I sharpen my claws & answer carefully. *Originally*, I say, *because colonization*. They tell me they need to read up on that. When I split in two, they don't understand, they speak louder & slower, they explain what should be done instead. *Where are you really from?* or *I don't see color.* I leave my brown legs & ass in a secret place & rise above, meaning aerial, bat's-eye view, inhaling through my nose & counting to ten. I come back & combine with myself. I fill in the bubble marked Other. I use a hyphen. In the Philippines, they deter me with seasoning: salt, garlic, ash; they reflect me ghostly on billboards, erase my melanin with papaya soap & Photoshop. Here, I am repelled by questions, mispronunciation, fetish, & the phrase *I know how it feels to be . . .*

ALL FILIPINA WOMEN ARE BEAUTIFUL

an old man with white hair says
to my brown, full-lipped face & I don't

know why, but it doesn't feel like a compliment.
When he says this, we're at the airport,

bags packed for a three-day flight & maybe
he's just asked *Where to?* I'm about four,

with crooked bangs & buck teeth, my lola
holding my hand in all the long lines. Maybe

she just smiles or thanks the man, after all
we all want to be maganda like the Filipina

Barbie on a friend's tall shelf: hair swept
into a shellacked knot, gold beaded dress

& her tiny waist clipped into the plastic stand.
I, too, think all Filipina women are beautiful

or should be, are supposed to be a certain kind
of beautiful like this Barbie, or photos I've seen

of Imelda with the same stiff wings
as sleeves. But they are not the same brown

-armed Filipina women I know that play pekwa
with my lola & bring fields of pancit, or the titas

in slippers taking jeepneys in the shadow
of a volcano. Instead, these beauties are fair

as the flesh crayon I use to color in everyone,
their lips painted pink, their eyes smoky

& tilted just so. And maybe I carry this with me
for years, watching Miss America pageants,

flipping through teen magazines, never seeing
myself, but watching my reflection

in the car's side-mirror, trying to tuck in my lips,
fold them against my teeth, thinner,

like the other girls at my school,
like the girls I see everywhere.

Your English Is Good

I served
their rice without
any spit even though
they thought they were funny saying
flied lice.

A pale,
bald man asks me
about his check. Who is
your server? I ask him. *I thought it*
was you.

The nice
couple turns mean
as fire when I mess up
their check. *Don't you dare!* the man spits
his threat.

When asked
their drink orders
they spoke slow & loud, then
impressed, complimented my good
English.

They ask
what kind of meat
is in these egg rolls? but
before I can answer they start
to bark.

GHAZAL FOR DOGEATERS

Someone yelled, *That dog gonna end up in a pot of rice!*
at Margaret Cho & she tells the story in her stand-up, as a joke.

When I waited tables, someone's dad ordered flied lice.
Someone's brother made a dog-meat-in-the-eggrolls joke.

In 1904, they shipped twelve hundred Filipinos, shivering in a
train car, from Seattle to St. Louis for a human zoo. No joke.

They forced them to eat twenty dogs a week: a spectacle
for the fairgoers. The butt of the joke. The root of the joke.

Once a co-worker barked like a dog because someone else
ate Chinese food; but calm down, it was just a joke.

When I told her it wasn't okay, she cried, called me a bully.
She asked me in tears, *Danni, why can't you take a joke?*

Five Hundred Years & Three Weeks Ago We Killed Magellan

In third grade, my Kentucky elementary school
taught me he was killed by savages
in the Philippines: picture a grainy textbook
photo of a man in a loincloth who looked

like my not-yet-30-year-old dad.
This fact unveiled itself during
our Explorers unit. We strung
yarn trajectories across all the oceans.

Here is where Pizarro went, Columbus,
Cortés. & Magellan's line cut & forever
ending on the archipelago of thousands.
When I heard it, one version of me

raised a little brown hand to correct
the teacher. In this universe, I begin
with *Actually*, & everyone turns
to watch, *His name was Lapu-Lapu*

& he was a hero. It's third grade, so I don't
yet know what a colonizer is, I don't know
that the rosary I receive for first communion
is a symbol of my own people's oppression.

I don't yet know how to correct a teacher.
What I really say is nothing & how I feel
is like the anonymous savage: rage
& heat & blood in my teeth, a simmering

under my brown skin. I know now
that Lapu-Lapu, the first Asian to resist

colonizers in history, stands 50 feet tall
in the capital city of Manila, holding

the kampilan, a weapon at rest. He looms:
symbol of our resistance & distrust,
reminder that we stand on legs
like immovable trees, rooted & ready.

How the Filipino Got Their Stereotype

—Another truth is that
sometimes people are hungry & poor,
sometimes there are dozens

of animals in the street doing nothing
but asking for food scraps
& if you don't even have the scraps

mango peels, old rice, fish bones—
what's to stop someone
from saving their own lives.

How to Resurrect a Chicken

My lolas sort organs under the mango tree: shiny, wet plums & beans; stuffing the empty body of a chicken. They push sharp, wet feathers into its skin, & sew its head to body with a knife. The older lola grabs its feet & dunks the body, head-first into a bucket of warm water. A bubble at the surface swims down to the bottom. The chicken swallows it & comes back to life, splashing. She pulls it out of the water, its feathers dry & neck bleeding, swings it onto the rock, under her slippered foot. She knocks the blood-rusted hatchet against the chicken's throat in soft taps. She holds a bowl of rice, soaked dark with purple blood, under the chicken's neck. Big grin & she tells me it's *chicken chocolate*. The chicken's neck wound gulps blood from the blade & bowl, the color from rice, bleaching it white & dry. The gash shrinks, pinches itself shut like an eye. She sets the chicken upright. It walks backwards, away from her, shaking its feathers into unruffled shape.

COUSIN DIVES HAS MORE, THIS TIME IN HER BOWELS

And before it was her ovaries. And before it was her breasts.
My tattooed arms remind her of the nipples they created: gathering skin

around the egg of her new breast, the color they buzzed needlewise.
Why do I need nipples? she asked me while I cut carrots into fingers.

No one will ever see them. Seventy-five years in a body she never shared.
And maybe this is what she said about the following subtractions.

Where Good People Live

We've got this circle of grass with an old American
sycamore spread a hundred or so feet wide, its branch arms
taking up space I learned not to. When it's a drought,

a neighbor's hose finds its way to the root-mouth
of the tree. *Someone really cares about that tree,*
my husband says. I learned last year that this neighborhood

was established as a whites-only space. A clause
in the deed made the homeowners promise to never
let a Black person live here. In 1987, my white

-passing mom & my dark-skinned dad bought a tiny brick
house here, its back pressed to the train tracks, dark
in the shadow of sycamores. It might be a fact

that we were the first to integrate this historically white
space. The promise not broken, but surely bent. Our melanin
meant for the Philippine sun, sallow in Kentucky winters. Years

& years before we saw another dark face. The skeleton beams
of a house where my little sister first met racism: some boys
throwing rocks & slurs, telling her to go back. Kids feared

my brown dad with the long ponytail & nicknamed him
The Cobra. A girl up the street couldn't play with me because
I *looked dirty.* There's a sign when you get here that names

our neighborhood, an acronym of the streets that make us up.
Wabash, Goodrich, Pensacola, Lackawanna: WGPL
claiming it's *Where Good People Live*, a shade different

from the original 1940s ads for these plots, bragging:
Only the best kinds of people will be approved.

EGGPLANT

when she tells me the story, it's him for sure, your dad, your dad got pushed, she says while oil pops. i always told him to push back, he didn't. i imagine she gave him this advice over a long-distance phone call, his fading voice lonely & small. he is always the boy in trouble for the bruises others made.

he tells the same story as somebody got pushed & fell on the eggplant. replaces himself with a nameless boy. all the cousins knew he was in trouble, their mouths in the shapes of shocked O's. the butt of his little shorts splits purple eggs open & spills tiny seeds like teeth in the dirt & soon he's taken by the wrist, inside to wash up & get guilt shaken over him. he says all he really remembers is how that eggplant grew the best, though i don't know if he means the fruit lost from its stem or the mother plant who was forced to let them go.

How My Dad Started Smoking

in front of the neighbors' house
is a bodega: bags of shrimp chips
clipped neon crunchy in a dangling
line, candies wrapped in squeaky
cellophane, cigarette boxes stacked

tidy & bright. my lola is peeling
the skin off frogs, her last cigarette
between her magenta lips & she squints
through smoke, *rené! go next door
& buy me another cigarette!*

my dad is ten, he drops
his fat pencil, used to answer
simple science questions
in capital-letter-print. he skips
in flip-flops to the neighbors' store,

raises a number one index finger
& brings the number two sign to his lips.
neighbors, who are also distant relatives,
give him a single white stick & strike
the match's red face against brown line

to light my lola's cigarette, nestled
in the branches of dad's peace sign.
he inhales smoke into his perfect pink lungs,
puffs once more & drags the smoke
like string across the yard.

1991 AND I RIDE TO CHURCH

after Lynda Barry

buckled into the brown vinyl car seat, its top like a tootsie roll. whitney houston is promising to always love me. sunday morning, early spring, the dew is frozen but the sun shines hard. my lola is driving, dashboard shining its silver letters, *corsica*. her leather gloved-hands on the wheel. to my right is the door that will crumple like tin foil when a motorcyclist slams machine & body against it in the bloody fog. in the back seat: kleenex box, umbrella, ice scraper, my lola's purse filled with rosy pink lipstick & red-striped peppermints.

QUINTOS

There's no pride in our name
because the man who left
it for us, sprinkling it on children
& women he abandoned, is not a man.

He is a black & white photo
& looks like a version of my dad
if he cut & slicked his hair: same brows,

same bony hands. He is standing
by a woman who sued him for polygamy,
the one he married while my lola
was pregnant with my dad, round

as a globe, fuming. I only wish
I could strip him of his Quintos,
make it belong only to the people

who love me to the marrow of my bones,
the ones who know my left-handed
handwriting, who show up
in its slanted poems.

THE OIL PAINTING THAT HANGS ON MY LOLA'S WALL

My imagined Philippines takes place in a painting: orange sunset mirror on the water, straw huts & carabao, something about rice swept in its hulls on the tile floor, a pot of rice over an outdoor flame. Salt, fish, heavy air & accent, dusk & itch, sweet diesel & smoke. This landscape is a feather, caught in the float between birdskin & concrete. I do not really know this place. I imagine my lola's stories in this setting—mudfish scales glinting in the cracks of floors & the burning smell of work & gasoline, the youngest of three sisters, their names so full of poetry. Cresenciana, Marcosa, & Remedios, a girl worn down by all the things she has to bear: this dim world & all the others before her.

Rosa de Rosario, 1929

The only photo of my lola's mother, Rosa,
sits in a gold, curved frame on her dresser
& always has. Rosa's round face looks
like mine, like my lola's, like my lola's sisters',

like my sister's. She holds a bouquet of white
roses & wears a dark terno with butterfly
sleeves, a pendant necklace, & rings. She stares
straight into the camera's eye, but I can't

quite tell if she's no-nonsense or about to
crack a smile. A crease in the photo divides her
in half at the waist, & as a girl I always thought
it was a waterline; that somehow this photo was

my great-grandmother in an impossible aquarium.
A spiky urchin sits at her feet & anchovies circle
her ankles. She is half-submerged & a fish-like tail
could be covered by her long skirt.

POSSIBLE REASONS MY DAD WON'T RETURN TO THE PHILIPPINES

1.
It was different when he could teenage
around in Arayat, blow smoke with cousins,
gulp tall, yellow beers. He has never been
an adult there. He'd walk into a house full
of new relatives, glassy skin lechón on the table
to celebrate his return. Cousins, nieces, nephews
requesting *Mano, po?* would line up
to press foreheads to his hand in bless.

2.
He might see a ghost, a father
he hasn't seen in 47 years. A familiar face
in a stranger: the man who delivers warm
& sweet pandesal on his bicycle with the same
long, straight teeth from my smile,
or an old man slouching smoke
into thick air on the curb. What if he asks
this man for a match & sees my sister's
eyes looking back at him? A face he once saw
in an old photograph.

3.
He has half-brothers, but that's all
anyone knows, not their names or what
their laughs sound like, if their teeth
are gapped, eyebrows thick. If the half
in common is a stranger, are you still brothers?

4.
What if he forgets how to do or say something:
Tagalog stale on his Kentucky tongue.
The people who raised him have disappeared
into a neighborhood of mausoleums. He has
one aunt left. Last winter she taught my sister & me
how to eat an Ilocano bean, its fibers
pulled through biting teeth.

5.
What if he remembers everything:
the rice balanced on a greasy thumb
& scooped into a mouth, the sour
bite of pink buro from a jar, pig shit
swirled in dust, house slippers
slapping tile before dawn,
the little boy in him left
here with all the cousins, no one
to call nanay or tatay, alone,
the shape of him on a mattress
the version of him that stayed.

PYTHON

she tells me people used to disappear in their village: grown men after nights
of drinking sweet whiskey & yellow beers, then the neighbor boy doesn't come
home for merienda, his siomai gone cold in a pool of sauce. then they found
it. she doesn't know how, maybe someone's foot got caught in a pomelo-sized
hole or someone saw the slither of tail descending into dirt & asked what
was that! maybe a shoe, empty of its foot, pointed the way like breadcrumbs.
down the road from where my dad grew up, some men started digging. they
beheaded it with shovels, unraveled a snake so big it ran the length of a house.
it could wrap around a jeepney. it could eat the village whole.

NOTES

In "Portrait of My Dad Through a Tent Window," "Ramirez" refers to "The Railroad Killer."

"Unbreak My Heart" takes its title from the 1996 Toni Braxton single.

"Scary Spice" refers to Mel B. of the Spice Girls. Ashland is the name of the plantation in Lexington, KY, owned by 19th-century Kentucky Statesman Henry Clay.

In "Age Eleven," the lyrics are from Alanis Morissette's "You Oughta Know" and "Hand in My Pocket" from her 1995 album, *Jagged Little Pill*. "*Dirty Dancing*" refers to the 1987 film, starring Patrick Swayze and Jennifer Gray. "Sweet Valley" refers to the *Sweet Valley High* series by Francine Pascal. "*Beauty and the Beast*" refers to the 1991 animated Disney film.

"Letter to My Childhood Crush" was inspired by a prompt from Tia Clark.

In "Who I Wanted to Be Instead," "*Something About Mary*" refers to the 1998 Farrelly Brothers' film *There's Something About Mary*, starring Cameron Diaz and Ben Stiller.

"Unpretty" takes its title from the 1999 TLC single.

The poems "Boobs" and "Pond's White Beauty" were inspired by Ellen Hagan's workshop from the 2014 Kentucky Women Writers Conference.

In "Breastfeeding," the final stanza ("Oh body,") is in conversation with Aracelis Girmay's poem "Kingdom Animalia" from her collection with the same title.

"Naptime Haibun" and "Pandemic Fall Haibun" were inspired by Aimee Nezhukumatathil's 2020 conversation with Tina Chang, Camille Dungy, and

Erika Meitner: "Motherland: Maternal Creativity and Balance in a Time of Quarantine."

The "Letters to Imelda Marcos" poems are from a project created for Adrian Matejka's Research in Poetry class. This project was largely informed by the 2004 documentary *Imelda: Power, Myth, Illusion*.

The poem "Milkfish" is based on a Cebuano folktale.

In "Pond's White Beauty," the phrase "sharp, pallid twin" refers to Zora Neale Hurston's essay "How It Feels to Be Colored Me," wherein Hurston claims, "I feel most colored when I am thrown against a sharp, white background."

The poem "Ghazal for Dogeaters" refers to the 1904 St. Louis World Fair and the exploitation of the Igorot people for a "human zoo." This poem was informed by the work of Janna Langholz. The Margaret Cho quote is from her 2000 stand-up special *I'm the One That I Want*.

The poem "Five Hundred Years & Three Weeks Ago We Killed Magellan" refers to the 500th anniversary of Ferdinand Magellan's death by Mactan chief Lapu-Lapu on April 15, 1521 in Mactan, Philippines.

The poem "Where Good People Live" refers to information gleaned from an Op-Ed written by Lisa Riddle in the July 2020 *Pensacola Park Post*.

The poem "1991 and I Ride to Church" was inspired by Lynda Barry's writing exercise from *What It Is*. The song referred to is Whitney Houston's 1992 version of "I Will Always Love You" from *The Bodyguard* film soundtrack.

Acknowledgments

Thank you to the editors of the following journals in which some of these poems first appeared, sometimes in slightly different form:

Anthropoid Collective: "1991 and We Flew for Days," "Cousin Dives Has More, This Time in Her Bowels," and "Possible Reasons My Dad Won't Return to the Philippines";
Best New Poets: "Pond's White Beauty" (as "White Beauty");
Cincinnati Review: "Unpretty";
Cincinnati Review miCRo: "Milkfish";
Cream City Review: "How to Resurrect a Chicken" (Finalist for 2020 Summer Prize) and "How the Filipino Got Their Stereotype";
Day One: "Cousins";
Mercado Vicente: "Letters to Imelda Marcos";
Mom Egg Review: "Trying";
Pluck! Journal of Affrilachian Art & Culture: "How My Dad Started Smoking";
Poetry: "First Milk," "Ghazal for Dogeaters," and "Self-Portrait as Manananggal."
Rabbit Catastrophe Review: "Portrait of My Dad Through a Tent Window" (Finalist for the Real Good Poem Prize);
Scrimshander Books: "Python";
Still: The Journal: "All Filipina Women Are Beautiful," "Who I Wanted to Be Instead," "Boobs," "Sixth-Grade Invisibility Studies," and "The Worst Part of Riding the Bus";
Toe Good Poetry Journal: "Quintos";

Several poems appeared in the ekphrastic chapbook *PYTHON* featuring photography by Shelli Quintos, published by Argus House Press. The poems, "Pond's White Beauty" (as "White Beauty") and "Portrait of My Dad Through a Tent Window" were included in *Black Bone: 25 Years of the Affrilachian Poets*.

Love and gratitude to my writing families: The Affrilachian Poets, Kentucky's Governor's School for the Arts, The Twenty, and my IU MFA cohort. Thank you for your kindness and generosity: Leslie Aguilar, Paul Asta, makalani bandele, Cathy Bowman, Stacey Lynn Brown, Su Cho, Bernard Clay, Debra Kang Dean, Teneice Durrant, Mandy Ellerbe, Scott Fenton, Asha French, Jaria Gordon, Dorian Hairston, JP Johnson, Peter Kispert, Kien Lam, Anni Liu, Amelia Martens, Yael Massen, Adrian Matejka, Jude McPherson, Dan Minty, Ife-Chudeni Oputa, Jeremy Paden, Joy Priest, Romayne Rubinas Dorsey, Ashley & Savannah Sipple-McGraw, G. A. Smith, Bianca Spriggs, Kayla Thomas, Ainsley Wagoner, Frank X Walker, Valerie Wernet, Keith S. Wilson, and Elle Wong. To the teachers who first heard me and helped me to feel seen: Ellen Hagan, Mitchell L. H. Douglas, Kelly Norman Ellis, Carole Johnston, Stephanie McDermott, Edwina Smith, Mary Tyng, Janet Geissler, Crystal Wilkinson, and Nikky Finney. To the writers I never met, but who nonetheless helped form these poems: Sandra Cisneros, Lynda Barry, Mary Karr, Li-Young Lee, Lucille Clifton, Ai, and Aracelis Girmay.

Special thanks with sprinkles on top to the writers who gave me their valuable time and feedback on these poems, in particular: Aimee Nezhukumatathil, Ross Gay, Lisa Low, J. Franck, and Tia Clark. I feel so lucky to be here with all your weird and beautiful brains, to be in community with you who teach me so much in all you write and make.

Giant thanks to the editors, designers, and staff at BOA Editions Ltd., who helped make my childhood dream come true, and took such care with my book: Peter Conners, Ron Martin-Dent, Genevieve Hartman, and Daphne Morrissey. Thank you, Justine Kelley for the gorgeous cover artwork.

I could not have made this book if it were not for the support and love of my family, both Quintos and Selby. Especially to my housemates and number one loves, Zach & Gus Selby: thank you for all you do, have done, and will do.

Thank you to my lola, Remedios Marcelo Bautista Quintos (Mima), for the stories.

ABOUT THE AUTHOR

Danni Quintos is a Kentuckian, a mom, a knitter, and an Affrilachian Poet. She is the author of *PYTHON* (Argus House, 2017), an ekphrastic chapbook featuring photography by her sister, Shelli Quintos. She received her BA from The Evergreen State College, and her MFA in Poetry from Indiana University. Her work has appeared in *Poetry, Cream City Review, Best New Poets, Cincinnati Review, Salon,* and elsewhere. Her knitting has appeared on the shoulders of many poets, writers, and artists, who are also friends and teachers. Quintos lives in Lexington with her kid & farmer-spouse & their little dog too. She teaches in the Humanities Division at Bluegrass Community & Technical College.

BOA EDITIONS, LTD.
THE A. POULIN, JR. NEW POETS OF AMERICA SERIES

COLOPHON

BOA Editions, Ltd., a not-for-profit publisher of poetry and other literary works, fosters readership and appreciation of contemporary literature. By identifying, cultivating, and publishing both new and established poets and selecting authors of unique literary talent, BOA brings high-quality literature to the public. Support for this effort comes from the sale of its publications, grant funding, and private donations.

❖

The publication of this book is made possible, in part, by the support of the following patrons:

Anonymous
Colleen Buzzard & Hucky Land
Bernadette Catalana
Christopher C. Dahl, *in memory of J. D. McClatchy*
James Long Hale
Margaret Heminway
Sandi Henschel
Nora A. Jones
Paul LaFerriere & Dorrie Parini
John & Barbara Lovenheim
Peter & Phyllis Makuck
Joe McElveney
Boo Poulin
Deborah Ronnen
William Waddell & Linda Rubel